FIND OUT ABOUT

animals

Steve Pollock

BBC

BBC Education
201 Wood Lane
London W12 7TS

ISBN 0 563 37333 4

Editor: Debbie Reid
Designer: Clare Davey
Picture research: Helen Taylor
Educational advisers: Su Hurrell, Samina Miller
Photographers: Paul Bricknell, Simon Pugh (photographs of people)
Illustrator: Salvatore Tomaselli

With grateful thanks to: Sue Carter and 'Bob and kittens', Jane Coney and 'Patti', Esme Davies and Julie Gallagher, Pascalle Matherson-Frederick, Christopher Vrahimis.

Researched photographs ©: **Bruce Coleman Ltd pp. 4 (bottom right), 5, 6, 10 (top), 11, 13 (right), 14, 16, 17 and 20 (top); NHPA pp. 13 (left), 20 (bottom), 21 and 22.**

Printed in Belgium by Proost
Origination by Goodfellow & Egan

Contents

These four animals are **different** from each other.
Look at the kind of **skin** or **body covering** they have.
What **differences** can you see?

fur

shell

feathers

damp skin

How are animals different?

Look at the cat and the tiger. They look different. But what can you see that is the same? They have the same kind of face. They both have fur or hair. They both have ears. They both have paws with sharp claws. They are both part of the cat family.

We are **different** from **cats**.
But we have **two** things that cats have.
Can you guess what they are?

A **frog** looks out for **danger** when it is hiding in water. What helps it to do this?

A **tiger** can **hide** in the tall grass. What helps it to hide?

Where do animals live?

Animals live all over the world. They live in lots of different places. The place where an animal lives is called a habitat. Tigers live in a habitat of tall grass or trees. The tiger's stripes help it to hide in this habitat.

Frogs spend part of their lives in ponds. The frog has its eyes, nose and ears at the top of its head. This helps it to breathe and look for danger while staying hidden in the water.

A **cat** lives with people. It needs certain **things** to live. Do you know what it needs?

A **cat** needs to be kept **warm** and have **toys** to play with.

toys

litter tray

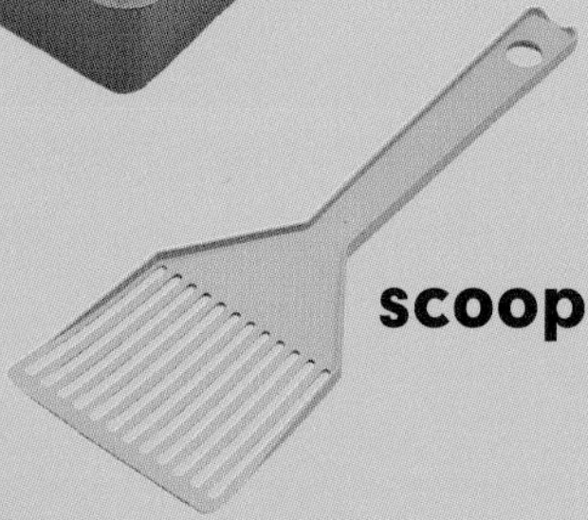

scoop

basket

feeding bowl

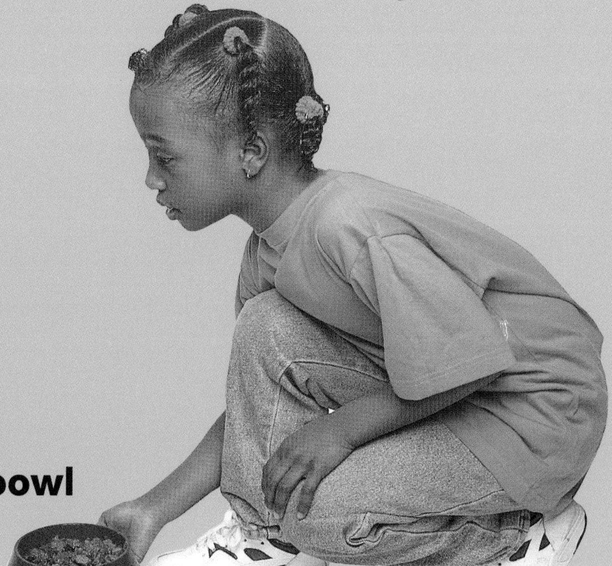

How should we look after animals?

All pets depend on people to live. Different pets all need the same things. They need food and water. They need a place to rest, which must be kept clean, and space for exercise too.

People care for their pets, but they do not always care for the habitats of wild animals.

Animals in the wild need a **proper** place to **live** too. People should not throw **litter** in this pond.

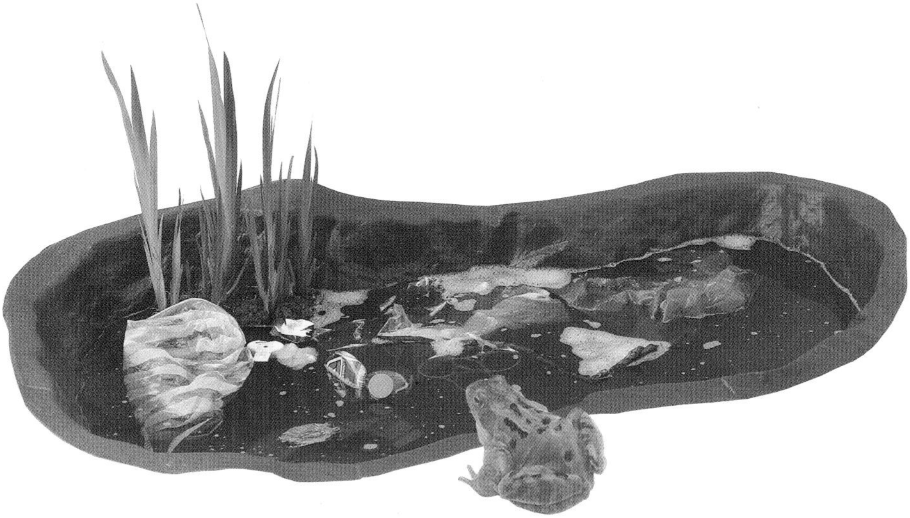

A **blue tit** likes **seeds, nuts** and **fruit**. It also eats insects.

A **snail** likes green **leaves**.

What do animals eat?

All animals must eat if they are to live. Some animals, like the snail, eat only plants. The snail feeds on green leaves. The blue tit eats both plants and animals. It feeds on seeds, nuts, fruit and insects.

Other animals, like the tiger, eat meat. The tiger must catch its meat. It is called a predator. The animals it catches and kills are called prey.

Tigers kill **prey** such as **deer.**

What helps this **cat** to **jump**?

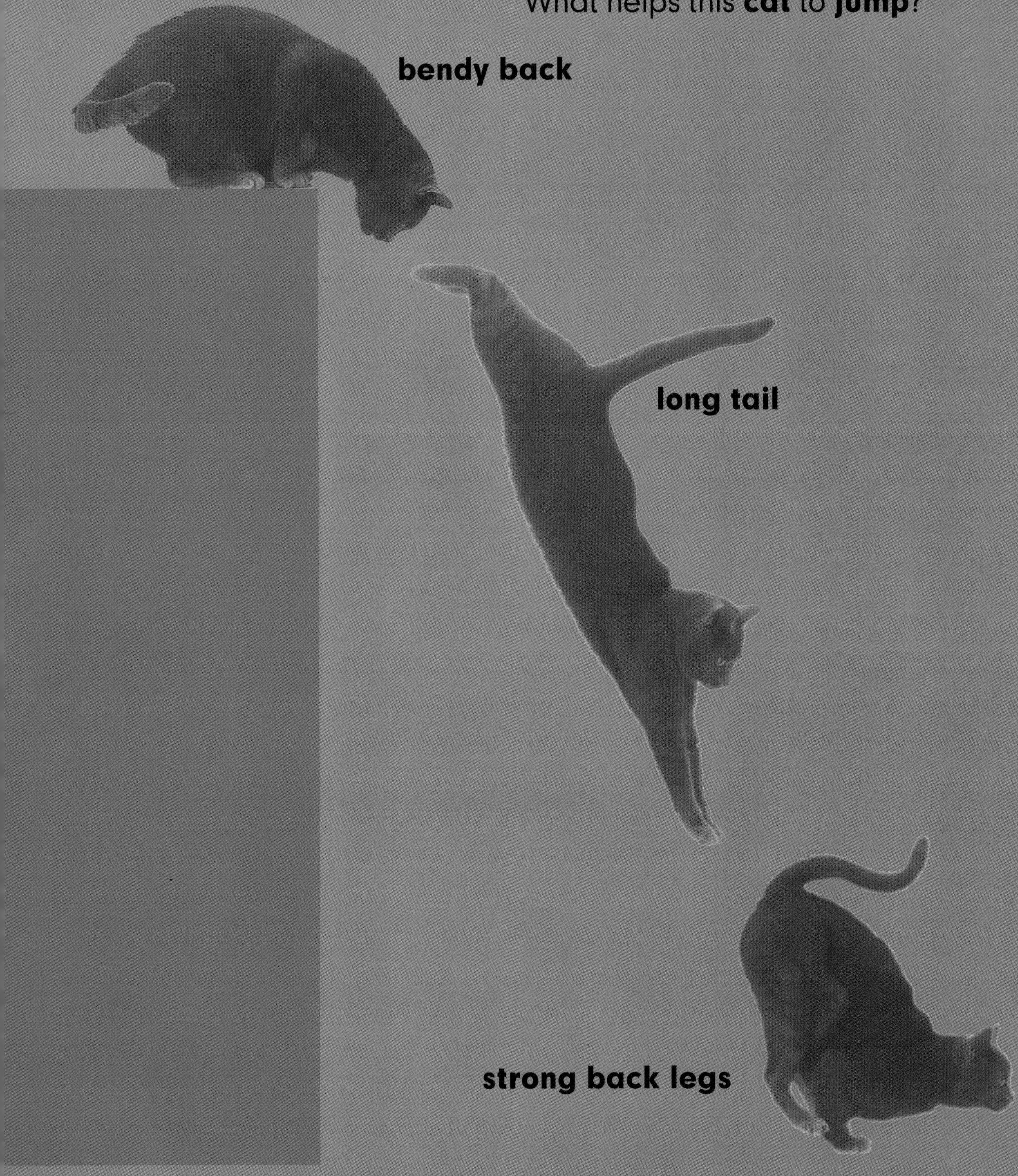

How do animals move?

Animals move around. How they move depends on what kind of animal they are. Look carefully to see which parts of the body an animal uses to move.

A cat uses its four legs. But what else helps it move? A bendy back and strong back legs help. Its body coils up like a spring which helps it to jump. A long tail helps it balance too.

What **parts** of the body help
this owl and this frog **move?**

What helps this tiger to **hear, see, smell, taste** and **touch?**

What senses do animals use?

All animals have five senses. A cat has five senses. These are seeing, hearing, smelling, tasting and touching. They help the cat find out what is going on around it. Look at the cat's face and work out which parts are used for which sense. These parts of the body are called the sense organs. Most animals have their sense organs on the head or at the front of the body.

For some animals, **one** sense organ may be more **important** than another. What is the **snail's** most important sense?

This **egg** has a hard **shell**. Inside the egg grows a **baby** blue tit.

baby blue tit

Baby blue tits have **hatched** from the eggs. They have to be **fed** by their **mother**.

What animals come from eggs?

Animals such as snakes, crocodiles and birds lay eggs. Growing inside the egg is a new animal. Birds lay eggs with a hard shell. The bird sits on the eggs to keep them warm. This is called incubating the eggs. After many days, the baby bird is ready to break through the shell. This is called hatching. After the chick has hatched it is ready to feed. Its mother helps it and protects it. When it is old enough it can look after itself.

Not all eggs are hard shelled. Not all mothers **look after** their eggs. After hatching, this young snail has to look after **itself** without its mother's help.

This cat has **babies** growing inside it.
It is **pregnant**.

The baby cats are called **kittens**.
They feed on milk from their mother.

What animals are born live?

Some animals give birth to live young. They do not lay eggs. Baby cats, called kittens, grow inside the mother cat. When this happens, the cat is pregnant. After nine weeks, the kittens are ready to be born. They are born blind and helpless. The mother licks them clean and looks after them. She feeds them on milk made in her body. When babies feed, it is called suckling.

People have babies too.
This baby needs to be **fed** and **looked after** by her **parents**.

A frog comes from an egg.
It **changes** many times as it **grows**.

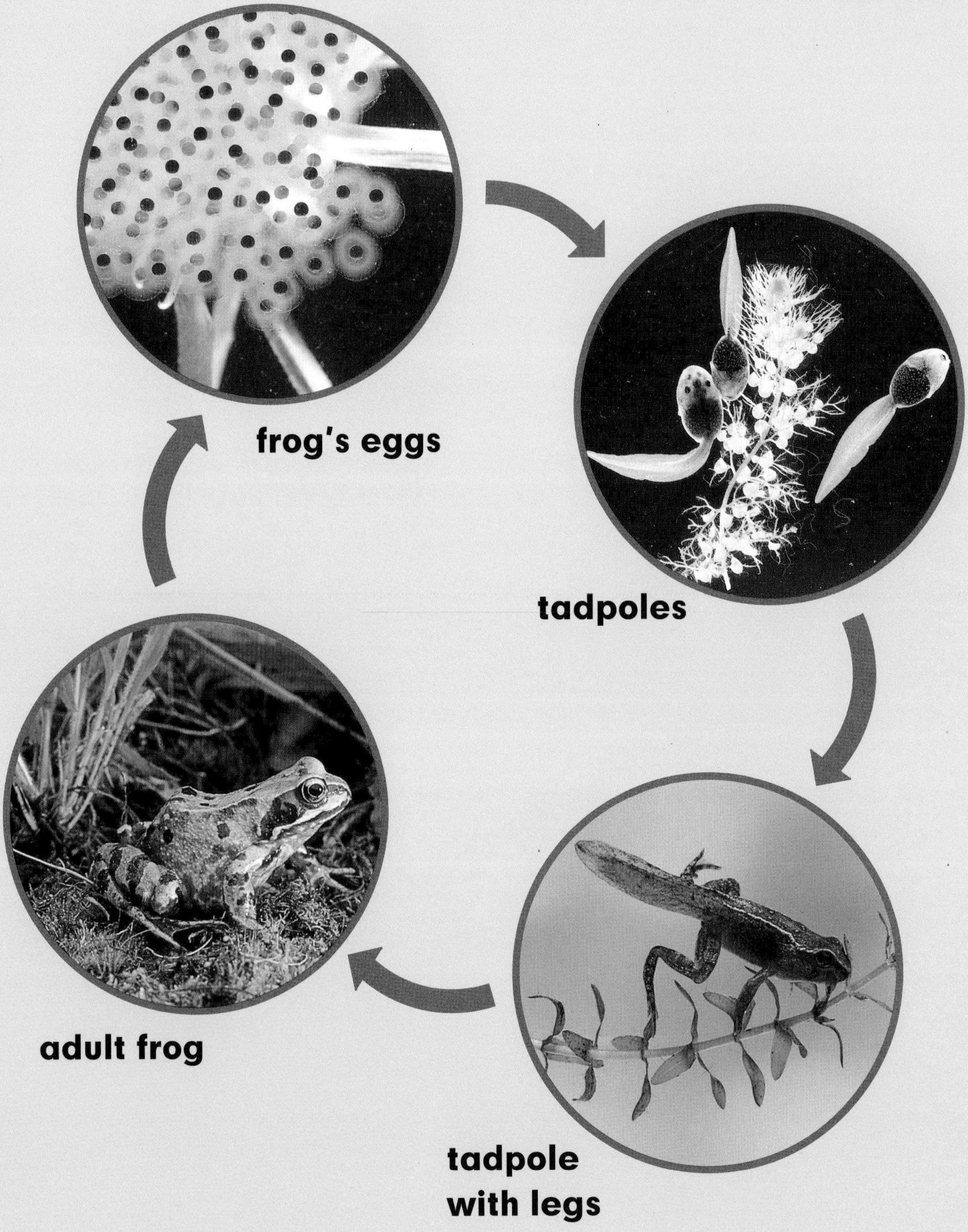

How do animals grow?

A frog goes through lots of changes as it grows. It starts off as a small, black dot in an egg. It hatches out as a tadpole. It looks nothing like its parents at this stage. As it grows bigger, it feeds on tiny animals in the water. It grows its back legs. Then, as it changes, its tail gets smaller. After twelve weeks, it is ready to leave the water and live on land.

Tiger cubs look like their parents when they are born.

This sign tells people in cars to be **careful** of **toads** on the road.

This owl has **killed** a mouse.

Why do animals die?

In nature, most animals die because one animal kills another for food. An owl is a predator. When a predator is hungry it must kill. An owl will kill and eat hundreds of mice each year.

Sometimes animals die by accident. The picture shows a special sign. This sign warns car drivers to watch out for frogs and toads crossing the road. It will help to save their lives.

Animals may get **sick** and **die**.
But animals that are well **looked after** and have enough **food** can **live** happily for many years.

Index

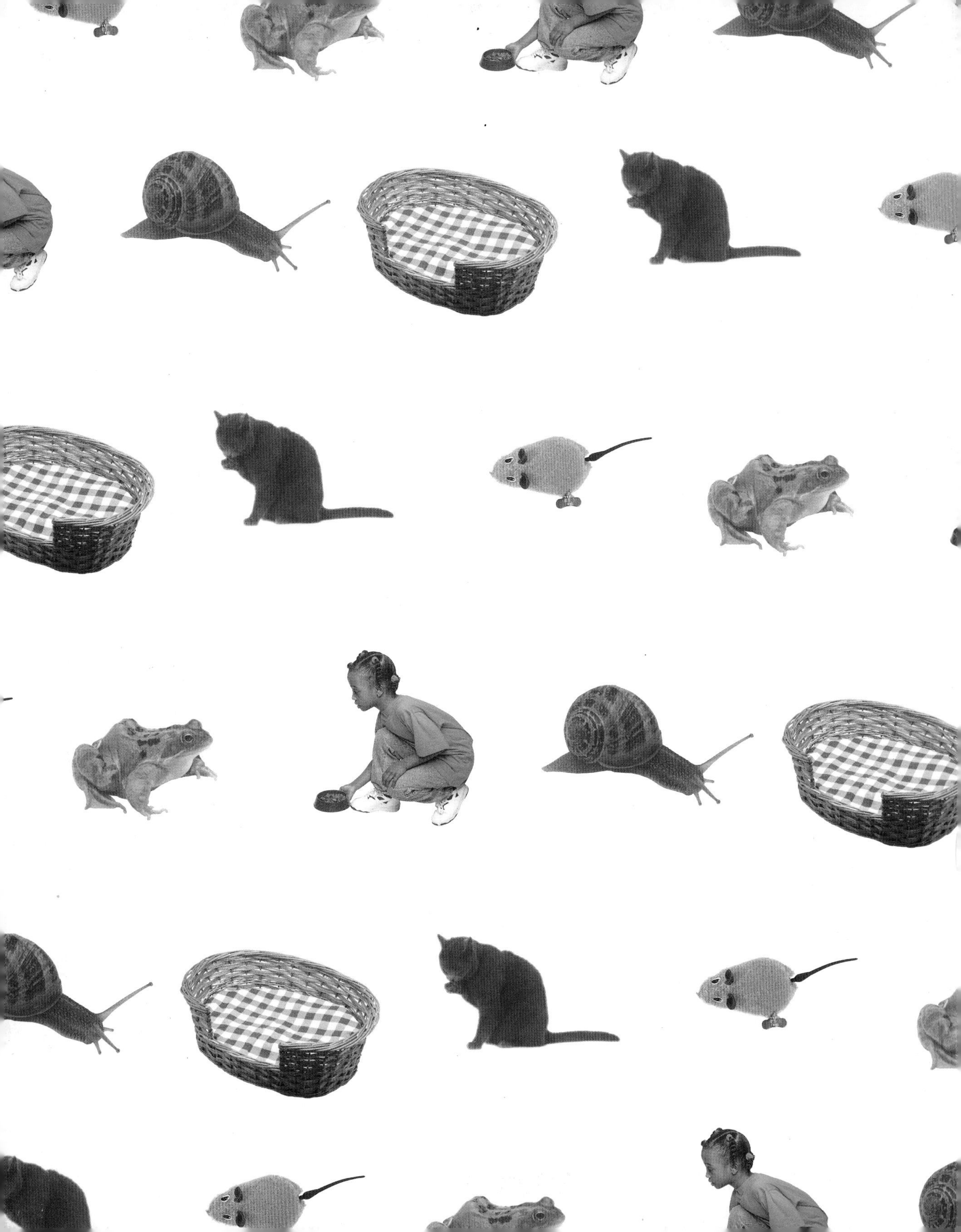